WriterSpark Academy's

Field Guide to Writing a Cozy Mystery Companion Workbook

By Melissa Bourbon

WriterSpark Academy's Field Guide to Writing a Cozy Mystery Companion Workbook

Print Book ISBN: 9798447740467

Published by Lake House Press

This book is dedicated to Annette Cutler and Trace Hartman, who have both been invaluable to this project, and so generous with their time. Thank you a million times over. ♥

And to everyone who has a story to tell. WriterSpark is for you.

Introduction

I started writing cozy mysteries by accident. I wrote a proposal for a mystery and my agent said, "Hey! Your voice would translate really well for cozy mystery. Have you ever thought about writing one?

My honest response was, "No. I don't know what a cozy mystery is!"

Fast forward fifteen years and close to thirty books. Now I know what a cozy mystery is.

Oh, how I wish I'd had a course like The Field Guide to Writing a Cozy Mystery or a workbook like this companion workbook to take me through all the planning steps. Writing a novel is hard work. It takes commitment and dedication not only to the act of writing, but to understanding and growing in your craft. That is why I created WriterSpark Academy, an online academy for new and aspiring writers to deepen their understanding of the writing craft.

For a lot of you—maybe most of you— writing is a passion.

But writing with the goal of publication takes hard work. It takes understanding the building blocks of a compelling story. But more than anything, it takes commitment and dedication to the goal.

WriterSpark Academy's Field Guide to Writing a Cozy Mystery is a Master Class during which students learn about everything that goes into crafting a cozy mystery. The course structures the hard work of writing a cozy mystery into achievable steps. It takes you through exercises and assignments to accomplish each specific genre story element. And it encourages you to make the commitment and dedicate yourself to the writing and publishing goals you've set.

Let me tell you about my writing background.

I'm a national bestselling author of multiple mystery series, and I'm also an Amazon #1 bestselling author. Before I was a writer, I was a middle school teacher. Once my writing career took off, I transitioned to teaching adults *the craft of writing.* I have worked with different online programs, and several continuing education programs, including Southern Methodist University's CAPE program and the Osher Lifelong Learning Institute with North Carolina State University. I've built a career in fiction writing, but I'm a teacher at heart.

I started my writing career not knowing anything. *Nothing!*

I set out to learn everything I could about the industry I wanted to be a part of, and about cozy mysteries, in particular.

Field Guide to Writing a Cozy Mystery is a course for anyone wanting practical guidance and activities that will lead to writing a cozy mystery because writing a mystery novel is serious business. I learned that early on. The fact is, you have to:

A) know how to construct a story and write a novel

B) know how to make that novel a murder mystery with intertwining plots, multiple suspects, the art of misdirection, and the planting of red herrings and clues in plain sight

C) become a detective so you can logically solve the crime

It took years for me to really hone my craft. I'm still learning, as I hope you will always be. We can always get better as writers. Anyone who says otherwise is dead wrong (pun intended!).

At the time of time of this publication, I've written and published 26 mystery novels in about seventeen years. Many of those novels are national and Amazon #1 bestsellers. Still, I am learning and growing as a writer.

Of those 26 novels, perhaps only two or three were a breeze to write. The rest took me through many ups and downs. Some characters didn't make the final cut. A handful of times the actual murderer changed in the end. Always, I've had moments when I wondered if I'd be able to pull the whole thing off.

The fact is, the better your understanding of the cozy mystery genre itself, as well as the basics of crafting a novel, the easier the writing process is. Even then, it's a challenge.

As an educator, one of the lesson plan design strategies I'm trained in is called backwards mapping. The basic idea is that you determine what, exactly, you want your students to have learned by the end of the lesson. From there, you work backwards, step by step, to determine the steps necessary to get to that end point.

When I write a mystery, I use the same backwards mapping strategy. As TS Eliot said: *"What we call the beginning is often the end. And to make an end is to make a beginning. The end is where we start from."*

Starting at the end is exactly what needs to happen when you're writing a mystery. You have to know what the crime is and how it was committed first, and only then can you start at the beginning to have your sleuth solve the crime.

It's also the method I've used to create the content for the Field Guide to Writing a Cozy Mystery Master Class online course. My goal is for each student in this course to come away armed with all the tools needed to craft a cozy mystery able to compete in the marketplace. Knowing this is the end goal, I worked backwards to create the content. From knowing all the details of the murder, potential suspects, and a compelling sleuth dogged enough to solve the crime all the way to the basics of crafting a scene, this course has it all.

The fact is, writing a novel is rarely an easy endeavor. Sure, you may have a killer idea, and you know you have what it takes to write that mystery novel. It'll be as easy as…murder.

In order to get to justice in the end, you first need to commit a crime. Only then can you start at the beginning, write the middle, and get to the end, which is the logical solving of the crime. And you have to do it all with with finesse.

There is never a guarantee of success, but I'm here to tell you that you can do it… and it can happen. I was (still am!) a mother of five, taught middle school Language Arts, and launched a successful career writing mystery novels.

If I can do it, you can, too!

From crafting the crime to creating a compelling sleuth, this Master Class takes you through the process of writing a cozy mystery. This workbook compiles all the support material for the activities, and the infographics, that are part of the online course, all compiled in one easy to use workbook. So get ready to commit murder.

You can find out more about WriterSpark Academy, our courses, and our 1:1 Coaching and Mentoring at https://writersparkacademy.com.

If you have enrolled in the course, make sure you join the WriterSpark's private Facebook group at: https://bit.ly/WS_FBGroup

WriterSpark Academy's website: https://bit.ly/WriterSpark

WriterSpark's Facebook Page: https://www.facebook.com/TheWriterSpark

Subscribe to the WriterSpark Newsletter: https://writersparkacademy.com/newslettersignup/

Happy Writing!

Melissa

Field Guide to Writing a Cozy Mystery Checklist

Introduction

- [ ] Mystery Spectrum
- [ ] Mystery versus Suspense
- [ ] Seven Rules of Cozy Mysteries
- [ ] Cozy Mystery Expectations
- [ ] Book Sleuthing

Digging In

- [ ] Case File: The Hook
- [ ] Case File: Investigative Deep Dive
- [ ] Case File: The Hook, Part 2
- [ ] Case File: The Cozy Setting

The Sleuth

- [ ] Dossier: Introduction and Appearance
- [ ] Dossier: Background/Childhood
- [ ] Dossier: The Sleuth's Family
- [ ] Dossier: Talents, Strengths, Skills, (Weaknesses), and Disparities
- [ ] Dossier: What would your protagonist do?
- [ ] Dossier: This or That?
- [ ] Dossier: Throwing your protagonist off-balance
- [ ] Dossier: Disparities in Your Sleuth
- [ ] Case File: Personality Traits

The Crime

- [ ] Case File: Mining Stories from the News_Examples
- [ ] Case File: Mining Stories from the News_Examples
- [ ] Case File: What If...?_Example
- [ ] Case File: What It...?_Blank

The Victim

- [ ] Dossier: The Victim's Appearance
- [ ] Case File: The Victim's Involvement_Examples
- [ ] Case File: The Victim's Involvement_Blank

The Villain

- [ ] Dossier: The Villain's Appearance
- [ ] Dossier: Villain's Childhood
- [ ] Dossier: Talents, Strengths, Skills, and Weaknesses
- [ ] Dossier: The Villain's Motive_Examples
- [ ] Dossier: The Villain's Motive_Blank
- [ ] Dossier: Who, What, When, Where, Why, and How
- [ ] Case File: Methods of Murder

Supporting Characters

- [ ] Dossier: Supporting Characters_Examples
- [ ] Dossier: Supporting Characters_Blank

Suspects

- [ ] Dossier: Suspects
- [ ] Dossier: Suspects_Example
- [ ] Dossier: Suspects_Blank
- [ ] Dossier, Truths and Lies

Clues and Red Herrings

- [ ] Case File: Clues and Red Herrings

Tying Up Loose Ends

- [ ] 6 Steps to Grabbing Readers with Catchy Back Cover Copy
- [ ] Case File: Back Cover Copy
- [ ] Case File: Furry Friends
- [ ] Case File: Cozy Template_Example
- [ ] Case File: Cozy Template_Example

Introduction

Mystery Spectrum
Mystery versus Suspense
Seven Rules of Cozy Mysteries
Cozy Mystery Expectations
Book Sleuthing

MYSTERY SPECTRUM

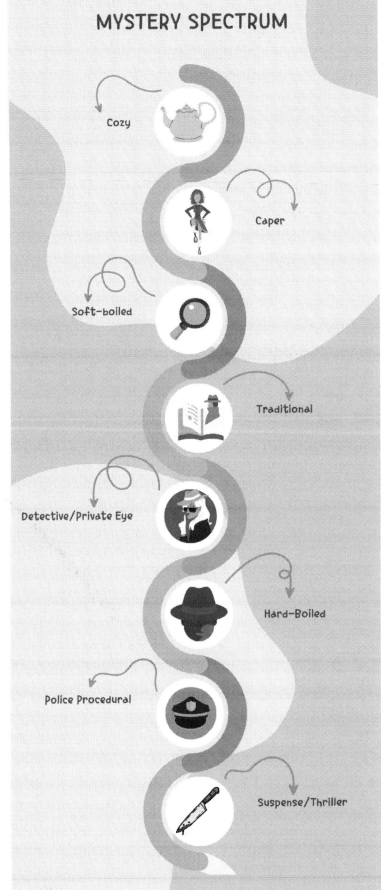

Cozy

Caper

Soft-boiled

Traditional

Detective/Private Eye

Hard-Boiled

Police Procedural

Suspense/Thriller

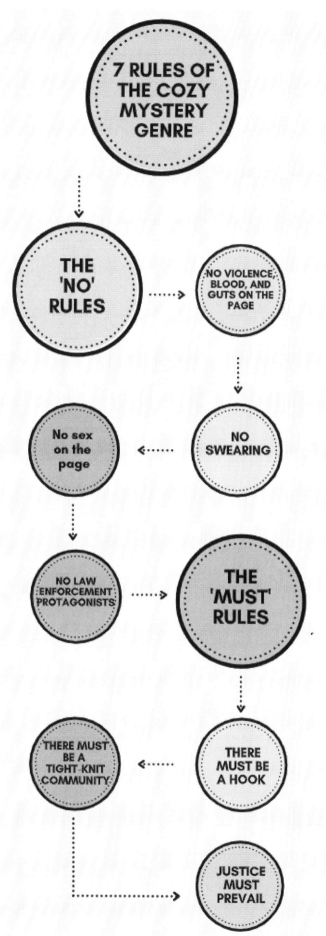

7 RULES OF THE COZY MYSTERY GENRE

THE 'NO' RULES

NO VIOLENCE, BLOOD, AND GUTS ON THE PAGE

NO SWEARING

No sex on the page

NO LAW ENFORCEMENT PROTAGONISTS

THE 'MUST' RULES

THERE MUST BE A HOOK

THERE MUST BE A TIGHT-KNIT COMMUNITY

JUSTICE MUST PREVAIL

MYSTERY

VERSUS

SUSPENSE

Mystery		Suspense
Mystery is a puzzle for the reader to solve alongside the sleuth		Suspense is an emotional rollercoaster from which the reader can't escape
Protagonist tries to identify a killer		Protagonist tries to catch the killer
Identity of the killer is unknown to the reader		Identity of the killer is known to the reader
Readers have only the information the sleuth has		Readers may have more information than the protagonist
Fair Play: clues are given so the reader can solve the mystery		No Fair Play: the reader has doubt about how it will all end
The puzzle helps drive the plot		Suspense helps drive the plot
Often told in 1st Person with just that POV		Often told in 3rd Person and/or has more than one POV character (including the villain)
The point of a mystery is to figure out whodunit		The point of a suspense is to stop the villain and bring him (or her) to justice

Cozy Mystery Genre Expectations

1 Super popular low-key mystery novels with little to no blood and guts

2 They feature an amateur sleuth

3 They center around a puzzle both the sleuth and the reader try to solve

4 Any sex is off the page (romantic subplots, yes, explicit sex, no)

5 They are typically set in a small town, neighborhood, or village

6 The sleuth's community plays a significant role in the story

7 They are usually part of a series and have a series arc

8 They have a 'hook' of some sort as a distinguishing feature of the series

9 Deductive reasoning, common sense, logic, and observation are used to solve the murder

10 By the end of the story, the crime is solved and justice has been served

Book Sleuthing

Before you start writing your cozy mystery, do a little investigative reading. This means reading with the intent of understanding how other authors craft their cozy mysteries. The goal is to look at these books through the lens of a writer rather than the lens of a reader

Follow these investigative steps to crack the cozy mystery code.

Step 1

Visit the library, a used bookstore, or your favorite retailer and get your hands on a good number of cozy mystery novels. Ten is good. Twenty is better!

Read them.

Step 2

Pay attention to:

- the introduction of the sleuth
- the discovery of the body
- pacing
- tone
- chapter length
- red herrings
- clues
- scene hooks

Step 3

Identify the point of view and analyze how it impacts the tone.

Most cozies are told in 1st Person, but that's not a hard & fast rule.

Think about the tone of the books you read. Which point of view and tone do you respond to. This should be the point of view and tone you target in your own writing.

Step 4

Break It Down

Choose one of the books you read and analyze it. Look deeply at the plot points, scenes & sequels, and characterization.

Create an outline to help you understand more fully how the author constructed the story.

Step 5

Do it again, this time with a cozy mystery you didn't love. Figuring out what doesn't work for you is just as valuable as learning what does.

Digging In

Case File: The Hook
Case File: Investigative Deep Dive
Case File: The Hook, Part 2
Case File: The Cozy Setting, Part 1
Case File: The Cozy Setting, Part 2

The Hook	The Competition	Pros & Cons

Notes

Villain	Victim	Motive	Secrets	Lies Told	Efforts to Misdirect

Notes

The Hook	How can I make my series different from the competition?

Notes

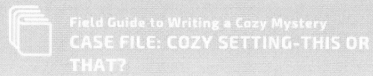

Types of houses (architecture)	Colleges
Wineries	Farms
Special businesses	Industry
Music venues	Festivals
Claim to fame for area	Pageants
Schools	School board
City council	Politics/Affliations
Gossip mill?	Coffee shops
Restaurants	Landmarks
Bridges	Types of trees
Other:	Other:

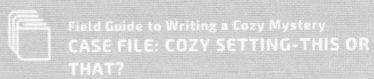
Winter Fall Spring Summer		Town/State/Country
Beach Desert Mountains Other		Region of the country
Rural Well-populated		Events Festivals
Demographics		Population density
Primary Religions/Churches		Other Religions/Churches
Historic markers		Town square? Downtown area?
Month(s) Weather patterns		How do people dress?
Trains/busses/transporation		General climate Terrain
Government influence		History of area
Ghosts or other superstitions		Prominent businesses
Bodies of water (lakes/rivers/creeks…)		Parks/forests/open spaces

The Sleuth

Dossier: Introduction and Appearance

Dossier: Background/Childhood

Case File: The Sleuth's Family

Dossier: Talents, Strengths, Skills (Weaknesses), and Disparities

Dossier: Disparities in Your Sleuth

Dossier: What Would Your Protagonist Do?

Dossier: This or That?

Dossier: Throwing the Protagonist Off-Balance

Case File: Personality Traits Inventory

Gender:

Age:

Hair Color & Texture:

Hair Style:

Ethnicity:

Skin Coloring:

Facial Hair:

Scars; Tattoos; Piercings:

Height & Weight:

Body Type/Bone Structure:

What Actor Would Play this Character?

Additional Identifying Features:

Additional Identifying Features:

Additional Identifying Features:

Parents:

Siblings:

Birth Order:

Home Town/City

Home (apartment, house, foster home...):

Educational Background:

Childhood Traumas:

Teenage Releationships:

Strongest Childhood Memory:

Childhood Memento:

Name	Relation to Sleuth	Identifying Traits and other Information

Notes

Inherent Skills and/or Talents:

Undiscovered Skills and/or Talents:

Strenghts:

Weaknesses:

Yet to be Discovered Weakness:

Yet to be Discovered Strength:

Things she Loves to Do:

Things she Hates to Do:

Think about how you will present your character to the world.	Now think characteristics hidden beneath the surface that are opposite or create dicotomy.

Receives the incorrect order at a restaurant:

Is the victim of catcalling:

Finds a wallet with an ID and cash on the road, with no one in sight:

Discovers a questionable credit card charge by her partner:

Receives a call to help a friend just as she's leaving for an important appointment:

Discovers her partner and best friend are having an affair:

Witnesses someone being racially offensive toward another:

Witnesses someone shoplifting:

Is seated on public transportation when a very pregnant woman walks in:

Learns that a neighbor was wrongfully acquitted of a rape charge:

Is alone at home at night when the doorbell rings:

Winter Spring	Fall Summer
Pizza	Burgers
A Mountain House	A Beach House
Television	Movies
Classical Music	Pop Music
Staying in on Saturday night	Going to a party on Saturday night
The city	The country
Reading books	Reading magazines
Working on a computer	Working with pen and paper
Coffee	Tea
Sweet	Savory

Who is your protagonist before your story begins? What major change has she undergone?

In what ways does this change challenge her? How does it throw her off-balance?

What does she want to be in her future? What is she striving for?

What obstacles are in her way? (i.e. Self-doubt? Money? Unfamiliar setting?...)

Identify the **POSITIVE** Personality Traits that best fit your protagonist:

Accessible	Conciliatory	Energetic
Active	Confident	Enthusiastic
Adaptable	Conscientious	Esthetic
Admirable	Considerate	Exciting
Adventurous	Constant	Extraordinary
Agreeable	Contemplative	Fair
Alert	Cooperative	Faithful
Allocentric	Courageous	Farsighted
Amiable	Courteous	Felicific
Anticipative	Creative	Firm
Appreciative	Cultured	Flexible
Articulate	Curious	Focused
Aspiring	Daring	Forceful
Athletic	Debonair	Forgiving
Attractive	Decent	Forthright
Balanced	Decisive	Freethinking
Benevolent	Dedicated	Friendly
Brilliant	Deep	Fun-loving
Calm	Dignified	Gallant
Capable	Directed	Generous
Captivating	Disciplined	Gentle
Caring	Discreet	Genuine
Challenging	Dramatic	Good-natured
Charismatic	Dutiful	Gracious
Charming	Dynamic	Hardworking
Cheerful	Earnest	Healthy
Clean	Ebullient	Hearty
Clear-headed	Educated	Helpful
Clever	Efficient	Heroic
Colorful	Elegant	High-minded
Companionly	Eloquent	Honest
Compassionate	Empathetic	Honorable

Identify the **POSITIVE** Personality Traits that best fit your protagonist:

Humble	Modest	Purposeful
Humorous	Multi-leveled	Rational
Idealistic	Neat	Realistic
Imaginative	Non-authoritarian	Reflective
Impressive	Objective	Relaxed
Incisive	Observant	Reliable
Incorruptible	Open	Resourceful
Independent	Optimistic	Respectful
Individualistic	Orderly	Responsible
Innovative	Organized	Responsive
Inoffensive	Original	Reverential
Insightful	Painstaking	Romantic
Insouciant	Passionate	Rustic
Intelligent	Patient	Sage
Intuitive	Patriotic	Sane
Invulnerable	Peaceful	Scholarly
Kind	Perceptive	Scrupulous
Knowledge	Perfectionist	Secure
Leaderly	Personable	Selfless
Leisurely	Persuasive	Self-critical
Liberal	Playful	Self-defacing
Logical	Polished	Self-denying
Lovable	Popular	Self-reliant
Loyal	Practical	Self-sufficient
Lyrical	Precise	Sensitive
Magnanimous	Principled	Sentimental
Many-sided	Profound	Seraphic
Masculine (Manly)	Protean	Serious
Mature	Protective	Sexy
Methodical	Providential	Sharing
Meticulous	Prudent	Shrewd
Moderate	Punctual	Simple

Identify the **POSITIVE** Personality Traits that best fit your protagonist:

Skillful
Sober
Sociable
Solid
Sophisticated
Spontaneous
Sporting
Stable
Steadfast
Steady
Stoic
Strong
Studious
Suave
Subtle
Sweet
Sympathetic
Systematic
Tasteful
Teacherly
Thorough
Tidy
Tolerant
Tractable
Trusting
Uncomplaining
Understanding
Undogmatic
Trusting
Uncomplaining
Understanding
Undogmatic

Unfoolable
Upright
Urbane
Venturesome
Vivacious
Warm
Well-bred
Well-read
Well-rounded
Winning
Wise
Witty
Youthful

Identify the **NEUTRAL** Personality Traits that best fit your protagonist:

Absentminded	Emotional	Ordinary
Aggressive	Enigmatic	Outspoken
Ambitious	Experimental	Paternalistic
Amusing	Familial	Physical
Artful	Folksy	Placid
Ascetic	Formal	Political
Authoritarian	Freewheeling	Predictable
Big-thinking	Frugal	Preoccupied
Boyish	Glamorous	Private
Breezy	Guileless	Progressive
Businesslike	High-spirited	Proud
Busy	Huried	Pure
Casual	Hypnotic	Questioning
Crebral	Iconoclastic	Quiet
Chummy	Idiosyncratic	Religious
Circumspect	Impassive	Reserved
Competitive	Impersonal	Restrained
Complex	Impressionable	Retiring
Confidential	Intense	Sarcastic
Conservative	Invisible	Self-conscious
Contradictory	Irreligious	Sensual
Crisp	Irreverent	Skeptical
Cute	Maternal	Smooth
Deceptive	Mellow	Soft
Determined	Modern	Solemn
Dominating	Moralistic	Solitary
Dreamy	Mystical	Stern
Driving	Neutral	Stoiid
Droll	Noncommittal	Strict
Dry	Noncompetitive	Stubborn
Earthy	Obedient	Stylish
Effeminate	Old-fashined	Subjective

Identify the **NEUTRAL** Personality Traits that best fit your protagonist:

Surprising
Soft
Tough
Unaggressive
Unambitious
Unceremonious
Unchanging
Undemanding
Unfathomable
Unhurried
Uninhibited
Unpatriotic
Unpredicatable
Unreligious
Unsentimental
Whimsical

Identify the **NEGATIVE** Personality Traits that best fit your protagonist:

Abrasive	Coarse	Discouraging
Abrupt	Cold	Discourteous
Agonizing	Colorless	Dishonest
Aimless	Complacent	Disloyal
Airy	Complaintive	Disobedient
Aloof	Compulsive	Disorderly
Amoral	Conceited	Disorganized
Angry	Condemnatory	Disputatious
Anxious	Conformist	Disrespectful
Apathetic	Confused	Disruptive
Arbitrary	Contemptible	Dissolute
Argumentative	Conventional	Dissonant
Arrogant	Cowardly	Distractible
Artificial	Crafty	Disturbing
Asocial	Crass	Dogmatic
Assertive	Crazy	Domineering
Astigmatic	Criminal	Dull
Barbaric	Critical	Easily Discouraged
Bewildered	Crude	Egocentric
Bizarre	Cruel	Enervated
Bland	Cynical	Envious
Blunt	Decadent	Erratic
Boisterous	Deceitful	Escapist
Brittle	Delicate	Excitable
Brutal	Demanding	Expedient
Calculating	Dependent	Extravagant
Callous	Desperate	Extreme
Cantankerous	Destructive	Faithless
Careless	Devious	False
Cautious	Difficult	Fanatical
Charmless	Dirty	Fanciful
Childish	Disconcerting	Fatalistic
Clumsy	Discontented	Fawning

Identify the **NEGATIVE** Personality Traits that best fit your protagonist:

Fearful
Fickle
Fiery
Fixed
Flamboyant
Foolish
Forgetful
Fraudulent
Frightening
Frivolous
Gloomy
Graceless
Grand
Greedy
Grim
Gullible
Hateful
Haughty
Hedonistic
Hesitant
Hidebound
High-handed
Hostile
Ignorant
Imitative
Impatient
Impractical
Imprudent
Impulsive
Inconsiderate
Incurious
Indecisive
Indulgent

Inert
Inhibited
Insecure
Insensitive
Insincere
Insulting
Intolerant
Irascible
Irrational
Irresponsible
Irritable
Lazy
Libidinous
Loquacious
Malicious
Mannered
Mannerless
Mawkish
Mealymouthed
Mechanical
Meddlesome
Melancholic
Meretricious
Messy
Miserable
Miserly
Misguided
Mistaken
Money-minded
Monstrous
Moody
Morbid
Muddle-headed

Naive
Narcissistic
Narrow
Narrow-minded
Natty
Negativistic
Neglectful
Neurotic
Nihilistic
Obnoxious
Obsessive
Obvious
Odd
Offhand
One-dimensional
One-sided
Opinionated
Opportunistic
Oppressed
Outrageous
Over-imaginative
Paranoid
Passive
Pedantic
Perverse
Petty
Pharisaical
Phlegmatic
Plodding
Pompous
Possessive
Power-hungry
Predatory

Identify the **NEGATIVE** Personality Traits that best fit your protagonist:

Prejudiced
Presumptuous
Pretentious
Prim
Procrastinating
Profligate
Provocative
Pugnacious
Puritanical
Quirky
Reactionary
Reactive
Regimental
Regretful
Repentant
Repressed
Resentful
Ridiculous
Rigid
Ritualistic
Rowdy
Ruined
Sadistic
Sanctimonious
Scheming
Scornful
Secretive
Sedentary
Selfish
Self-indulgent
Shallow
Shortsighted
Shy

Silly
Single-minded
Sloppy
Slow
Sly
Small-thinking
Softheaded
Sordid
Steely
Stiff
Strong-willed
Stupid
Submissive
Superficial
Superstitious
Suspicious
Tactless
Tasteless
Tense
Thievish
Thoughtless
Timid
Transparent
Treacherous
Trendy
Troublesome
Unappreciative
Uncaring
Uncharitable
Unconvincing
Uncooperative
Uncreative
Uncritical

Unctuous
Undisciplined
Unfriendly
Ungrateful
Unhealthy
Unimaginative
Unimpressive
Unlovable
Unpolished
Unprincipled
Unrealistic
Unreflective
Unreliable
Unrestrained
Unself-critical
Unstable
Vacuous
Vague
Venal
Venomous
Vindictive
Vulnerable
Weak
Weak-willed
Well-meaning
Willful
Wishful
Zany

The Crime

Case File: Mining Stories from the
News_Examples
Case File: Mining Stories from the News_Blank
Case File: What if…?_Examples
Case File: What if…?_Blank

Example: Funeral home director investigated for harvesting body parts and selling them.

Example: Boarding house landlady (The Death House Landlady) has been killing elderly and mentally disabled boarders for their Social Security money.

Example: Serial killer found hiding out in a nudist resort

Example: Art Car show.

Example: Bonnie and Clyde

What if a deceased man is the victim of a funeral home director's skeezy plan to harvest organs?

What if a local man disappears without a trace, and a connection is made to a landlady and her boarding house?

What if a drug operation is being run from a nudist resort?

What if a man is found dead in the art car he finished, just before the big parade?

What if Bonnie and Clyde left something hidden in a house they stayed in and now someone is killed because of it?

CRIME NOTES: _____

_____

_____

_____

_____

_____

_____

_____

_____

_____

_____

_____

_____

_____

_____

_____

_____

_____

_____

_____

_____

_____

The Victim

Dossier: The Victim's Appearance
Case File: The Victim's Involvement_Examples
Case File: The Victim's Involvement_Blank

Name:

Gender:

Age:

Ethnicity:/Slin Color:

Hair Style:

Facial Hair, Tattoos, Scars, Piercings:

Body Type/Bone Structure:

Height & Weight:

Connection to the Protagonist:

One Secret he/she has:

One Secret he/she has:

One Secret he/she has:

Additional Identifying Features:

Additional Identifying Features:

What Actor Would Play this Character?

What if...?

What if a deceased man is the victim of a funeral home director's skeezy plan to harvest organs?

What if a local man disappears without a trace, and a connection is made to a landlady and her boarding house?

What if a drug operation is being run from a nudist resort?

What if a man is found dead in the art car he finished, just before the big parade?

What if Bonnie and Clyde left something hidden in a house they stayed in and now someone is killed because of it?

Notes:

How is the victim involved?

The victim's middle aged daughter figures out that something isn't right. She has to be killed to keep her quiet.

The missing man witnessed the digging of a grave in the backyard of the landlady. He has to be killed to keep him quiet.

The drugs are being distributed through a professional ball team's trainer. He becomes a liability so he must be killed.

The victim isn't well-liked. He's killed because of some shady dealings and people he's wronged. The art car is where place he's found.

A man plays Santa at a historic house event so he can search for the hidden treasure, but he interrupts someone else searching for the same thing.

What if...?

How is the
victim involved?

Notes:

The Villain

Dossier: The Villain's Appearance

Dossier: Villain's Childhood

Dossier: Talents, Strengths, Skills, and Weaknesses

Dossier: The Villain's Motive_Examples

Dossier: The Villain's Motive_Blank

Dossier: Who, What, When, Where, Why, and How

Case File: Methods of Murder

Gender:

Age:

Hair Color & Texture:

Hair Style:

Ethnicity:

Skin Coloring:

Facial Hair:

Scars; Tattoos; Piercings:

Height & Weight:

Body Type/Bone Structure:

What Actor Would Play this Character?

Additional Identifying Features:

Additional Identifying Features:

Additional Identifying Features:

Parents:

Siblings:

Birth Order:

Home Town/City

Home (apartment, house, foster home...):

Educational Background:

Childhood Traumas:

Teenage Releationships:

Strongest Childhood Memory:

Childhood Memento:

Inherent Skills and/or Talents:

Undiscovered Skills and/or Talents:

Strenghts:

Weaknesses:

Yet to be Discovered Weakness:

Yet to be Discovered Strength:

Things she Loves to Do:

Things she Hates to Do:

What if...?

Involved how.?

What if a deceased man is the victim of a funeral home director's skeezy plan to harvest organs?

The victim's middle aged daughter figures out that something isn't right.

The villain's motive: The owner of the funeral home needs to stop the woman from blowing the whistle on his body harvest business.

What if a local man disappears without a trace, and a connection is made to a landlady and her boarding house?

The missing man witnessed the digging of a grave in the backyard of the landlady.

The villain's motive: The landlady poisons the man to keep him quiet.

What if a drug operation is being run from a nudist resort?

The drugs are being distributed through a professional ball team's trainer. The trail leads to the nudist resort.

The villain's motive: The victim decided to sell drugs on his own, undercutting the bigger operation.

What if a man is found dead in the art car he finished, just before the big parade?

The victim isn't well-liked. He's killed because of some shady dealings. The art car is just the place he's found.

The villain's motive: The victim swindled a group of people in a land development deal. One of them kills out of revenge.

What if Bonnie and Clyde left something hidden in a house they stayed in and now someone is killed because of it?

A man plays Santa at a historic house event so he can search for the hidden treasure, but he interrupts someone else searching for the same thing.

The villain's motive: The victim gets in the way of the villain finding the treasure. He kills to get the man out of the way.

What if...?

Involved how.?

The villain's motive:

The villain's motive:

The villain's motive:

The villain's motive:

The villain's motive:

Who is the victim?

What is the motive?

When does the murder occur?

Where does the murder occur?

Why does the villain resort to murder?

How is the murder committed?

Methods of Murder

Asphyxiation/Suffocation
- Smothering
- smoke inhalation
- Car exhaust

Poisoning
- Ingesting poisonous plant material (fungi, nightshades, hemlock, foxglove...)
- Ingesting other poisons: (arsenic, antifreeze. strychnine, asbestos, insulin...)

Bludgeoning
- Use of a heavy object

Buried Alive

Drowning

Hanging

Car Accident

Knife (severing artery/stabbing)

Stabbing (various tools)

Strangulation

Supporting Characters

Dossier: Supporting Characters_Examples
Dossier: Supporting Characters_Blank

Field Guide to Writing a Cozy Mystery
DOSSIER: SUPPORTING CHARACTERS
SIDE-KICK; ROMANTIC INTEREST; TRUSTED FRIEND; OPPOSITION

Name	Type of Supporting Character	Identifying Traits and other Information
Daisy Santiago	Trusted Friend	Curly hair, short, librarian, boisterous, Latina
Ruby Monroe	Trusted Friend	Owns Devil's Brew, has niece Sasha, Romance with Grey, Black
Hattie Juniper Pickle	Side-kick & Trusted Friend	Knew Cassie & Leo, lives across the street, eccentric, blue hair, unlit cig, trike (Rizzo), knows everyone
Cyrus McAdams	Trusted Friend	Knew Cassie & Leo, Jamie's grandfather, co-owner of the bookshop, mentor
Jamie McAdams	Romantic Interest & Trusted Friend	Co-owner of the bookshop, super smart, medieval Irish history, crazy about Ivy
Grey Hawthorne	Side-kick & Trusted Friend	Pippin's twin, doubts the curse, interested in Ruby, sailor, fisherman, loves the water, woodworkder

Notes

Name	Type of Supporting Character	Identifying Traits and other Information

Notes

Name	Type of Supporting Character	Identifying Traits and other Information

Notes

Suspects

Dossier: Suspects
Dossier: Suspects_Example
Dossier: Suspects_Blank
Dossier: Truths and Lies

Name	General Information	Personality Traits & Quirks
	Age: Gender: Occupation:	Notable personality traits: Favorite expressions: Identifying mannerisms:
	Age: Gender: Occupation:	Notable personality traits: Favorite expressions: Identifying mannerisms:
	Age: Gender: Occupation:	Notable personality traits: Favorite expressions: Identifying mannerisms:

Murder Victim:

Name	Role in Story	Secrets, Identifying Traits and other Information
Hugh	Mysterious man who shows up at Pippin's house, and then summons her to the library	A descendant of Titus, translucent eyes, very mysterious, Hugh isn't his real name, Pippin doesn't know if she can trust him. Secret: Isn't connected only through Titus
Jed Riordin	Old friend of Leo's, knows things about the curse, says he's a friend and that he helped Leo 20 years ago	Part of the men's discussion group, knew the victim, was present just before the murder in the bookshop. Secret: Knew Aunt Rose and Cora at Cape Misery Secret: has a child

Murder Victim:

Name	Connection to Victim	Secrets, Identifying Traits and other Information
	Motive:	
	Motive:	
	Motive:	

Murder Victim:

Name	Two Truths or Two Lies	One Lie or One Truth

Notes

SUSPECT NOTES:_____

_____

_____

_____

_____

_____

_____

_____

_____

_____

_____

_____

_____

_____

_____

_____

_____

_____

Clues and Red Herrings

Case File: Clues and Red Herrings

Potential Clues	Potential Red Herrings

Notes

Tying Up Loose Ends

6 Steps to Grabbing Readers with Catchy Back
Cover Copy

Case File: Back Cover Copy

Case File: Furry Friends

Case File: Cozy Template_Example

Case File: Cozy Template_Blank

Case File: Subplot Elements

Case File: Trail of Clues

6 *Steps* to Grabbing Readers with Catchy Back Cover Copy

Back cover copy goes on the back of your book and on your book's retail page. Use all six of these tactics to entice readers.

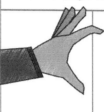

Hook them early.

This is not your series theme. This is a one or two sentence hook about your story to grab readers' attention. It often involves a pun connected to the theme.

Introduce the protagonist.

Who is the amateur sleuth who will carry the story? Give her name and the life conflict she faces at the beginning of the series.

Show what her future could hold.

Her chance for success or happiness is within reach in her new world.

Introduce the conflict.

Show the disruption of the protagonist's new life with a murder.

Give the stakes.

What happens if the protagonist doesn't solve the crime?

Make it punny.

Make sure there are puns and/or figurative language connecting the copy to series hook (theme).

The Hook	
Introduce the Protagonist	
Show the potential future	
Introduce the Conflict (murder)	
Raise the Stakes	
Make it Punny	

Type	Breed	Identifying Features	Personality Traits	Name

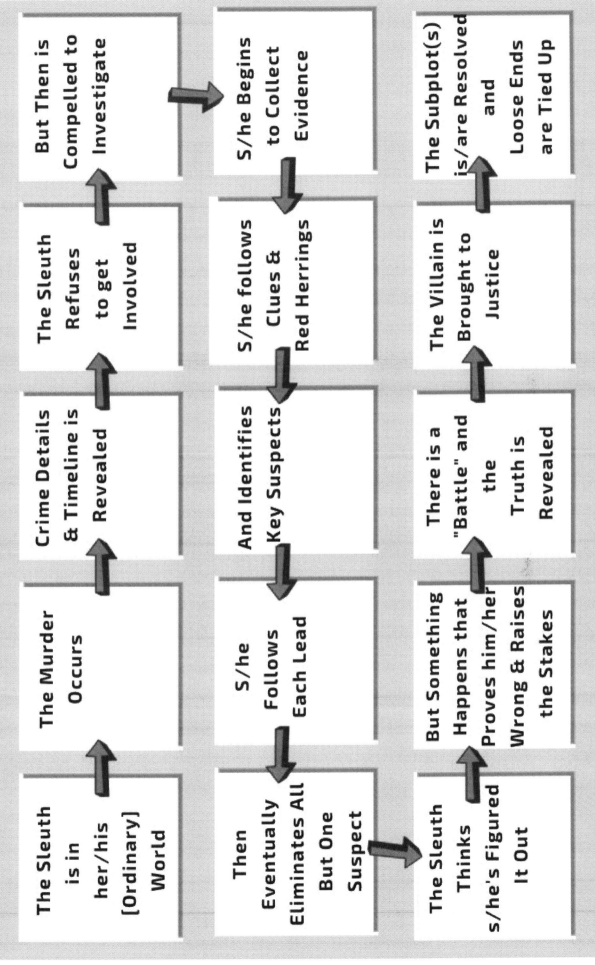

The Sleuth is in her/his [Ordinary] World

The Murder Occurs

Crime Details & Timeline is Revealed

The Sleuth Refuses to get Involved

But Then is Compelled to Investigate

S/he Begins to Collect Evidence

S/he follows Clues & Red Herrings

And Identifies Key Suspects

S/he Follows Each Lead

Then Eventually Eliminates All But One Suspect

The Sleuth Thinks s/he's Figured It Out

But Something Happens that Proves him/her Wrong & Raises the Stakes

There is a "Battle" and the Truth is Revealed

The Villain is Brought to Justice

The Subplot(s) is/are Resolved and Loose Ends are Tied Up

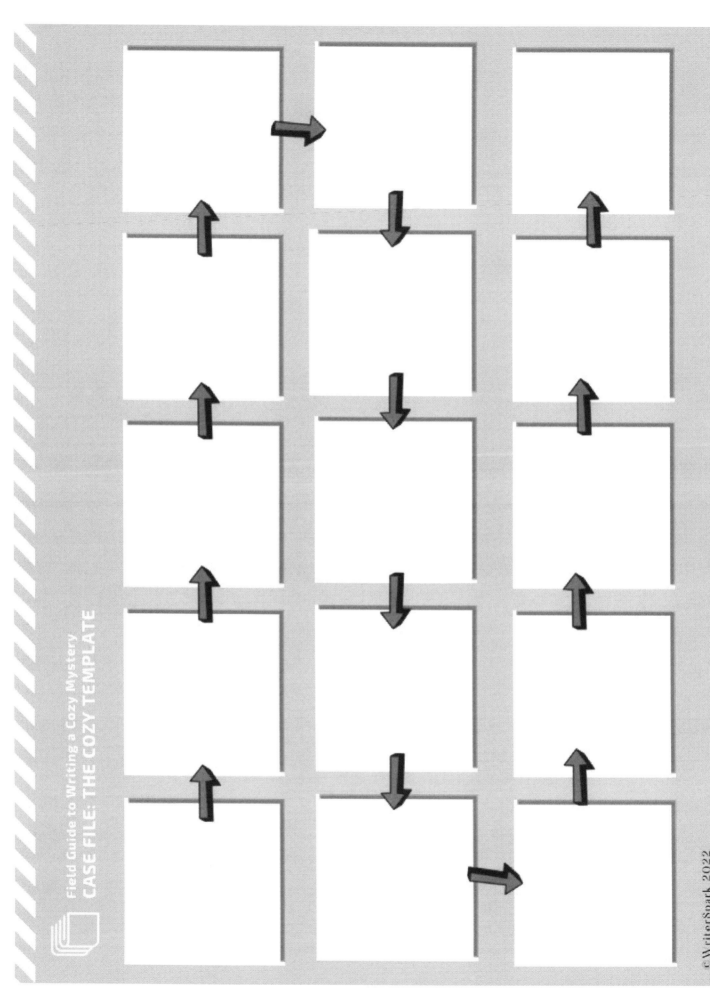

Romantic Subplot

Personal Subplot

Other Subplot

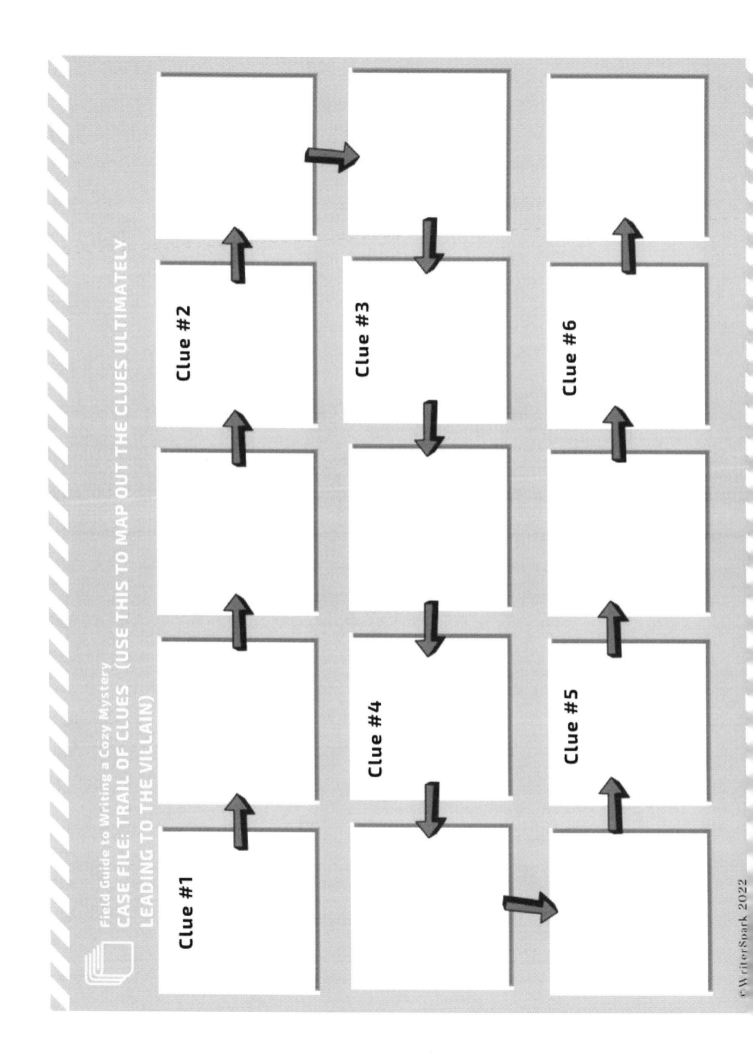

Field Guide to Writing a Cozy Mystery
CASE FILE: TRAIL OF CLUES (USE THIS TO MAP OUT THE CLUES ULTIMATELY
LEADING TO THE VILLAIN)

Clue #1

Clue #2

Clue #3

Clue #4

Clue #5

Clue #6

©WriterSpark 2022

NOTES:

NOTES:

NOTES:

NOTES:

NOTES:

NOTES:

NOTES:

NOTES:

Acknowledgements

Creating WriterSpark Academy has been a labor of love, and is my way of paying it forward to other new and aspiring writers who want to learn more about writing a cozy mystery

This course and Companion Workbook is due, in great part, to Judy Taylor of Webbability and JT Dataworks. When I contemplated the scale of what I wanted to create with WriterSpark Academy she was there to encourage and guide me.

I also want to give a big thanks to my dad, Bruce Bourbon, who is always there as a sounding board and mentor, and to my mom, Marilyn Sears Bourbon, who has always been my biggest fan.

The writing community is small, and I'm so grateful for so many people who have become my people. This book is dedicated to Annette Cutler and Trace Hartman, who have both been invaluable and so generous with their time.

Finally, I couldn't do what I do—writing books and teaching writing—without the support of my husband, Carlos Ramirez, who has always been in my corner to encourage and support my many creative endeavors. And to Bean, Dobby, and Pippin, my shadows and constant companions.

About the Author

Melissa Bourbon is the national bestselling author of more than 26 mystery books, including the Book Magic Mysteries, the Lola Cruz Mysteries, A Magical Dressmaking Mystery series, the Bread Shop Mysteries, written as Winnie Archer.

She is a former middle school English teacher who gave up the classroom in order to live in her imagination full time. Melissa, a California native who has lived in Texas and Colorado, now calls the southeast home. She hikes, practices yoga, cooks, and is slowly but surely discovering all the great restaurants in the Carolinas. Since her five amazing kids are living their lives, scattered throughout the country, her dogs, Bean, the pug, Dobby, the chug, and Pippin, a rescue puppy, keep her company while she writes.

Melissa lives in North Carolina with her educator husband, Carlos. She is beyond fortunate to be living the life of her dreams.

Books by Melissa Bourbon

Book Magic Mysteries

The Secret on Rum Runner's Lane

Murder in Devil's Cove

Murder at Sea Captain's Inn

Murder Through an Open Door

Murder and an Irish Curse

Bread Shop Mysteries,

written as Winnie Archer

Kneaded to Death

Crust No One

The Walking Bread

Flour in the Attic

Dough or Die

Death Gone a-Rye

A Murder Yule Regret

Bread Over Troubled Water

Magical Dressmaking Mysteries

Pleating for Mercy

A Fitting End

Deadly Patterns

A Custom-Fit Crime

A Killing Notion

Printed in Great Britain
by Amazon